Keys to a Winning Attitude

26 Ways to Have a Positive Mindset

LESLEY NARDINI

WHAT OTHERS ARE SAYING ABOUT LESLEY NARDINI

"The ideas and information in this book will help business of every size."

Kevin Harrington, Original Shark on
Hit TV Show, *Shark Tank*
Inventor of the Infomercial ($4B in sales on TV)

"Lesley's book is full of information and simple ideas that will delight and surprise on a consistent basis!"

Joe Theismann, Legendary NFL World
Champion Quarterback
NFL Football TV Commentator
Featured on the Hit Movie, *The Blind Side*

"Lesley is a dynamic speaker and author who will educate and motivate your group to new levels of success. Bottom line – this book ROCKS!"

Craig Duswalt, Speaker, Author, Radio Host
Creator of *RockStar Marketing*
www.CraigDuswalt.com

"This terrific book is loaded with practical proven ideas!"
Brian Tracy, Legendary Speaker, Author,
Trainer & Consultant
Top Selling Author of 70 Books
Spoken for 5,000,000 people in 73 Countries

"Lesley is an amazing speaker, author and business leader. I love her book! If you're ready to achieve more business success, then read and absorb the strategies in this brilliant book by my friend Lesley Nardini!"
James Malinchak, Featured ABCs Hit
TV Show, *Secret Millionaire*
Top-Selling Author, *Millionaire Success Secrets*
Founder, www.MillionaireFreeBook.com

"This book is the secret weapon that everyone can use to achieve the success they are looking for. Lesley has put together a collection of unforgettable tips and easy to use strategies that are incredibly noteworthy and valuable. I am recommending this book to every one of my clients across the globe."
John Formica, The "Ex-Disney Guy"
America's Customer Experience Speaker and Coach
www.JohnFormica.com

"Lesley truly offers a unique blend of success skills while inspiring. This book is such a valuable and practical guide for everyone."

Forbes Riley, "The Queen of Selling on TV" Hosted 140+ National TV Shows & Infomercials

"A practical guide with relevant examples of how to be exceptional."

Jill A. Lublin, 3x Best Seller, International Speaker CEO, www.JillLublin.com

"Lesley's book is amazing and one of the BEST. This is a must read that will provide you with immediate winning action ideas."

Steven R. Shallenberger, Founder, Author, National Bestseller of *Becoming Your Best: The 12 Principles of Highly Successful Leaders*

Lesley was a wonderful, motivational speaker for our ELEVATE Leadership conference. Her specialty is being your best and being in control of your own destiny. We hired her as our Keynote speaker and wouldn't hesitate to recommend her.

Karon Paul, VP Human Resources, Guardian Real Estate Services

MOTIVATE AND INSPIRE OTHERS!
More Books by Lesley Nardini

$24.95 Retail

Lesley spent 30 years working as a customer service professional in the banking and hospitality industries where she won numerous awards for outstanding customer service. During that time, she learned that the key to exceptional customer service is caring about people and providing a personal touch. In this book you'll learn simple ways to make your customers feel valued and appreciated so that your company will stand out from all the competition.

$12.95 Retail

This book is a compilation of quotes for women, by women that will give you courage, strength and confidence. You'll find quotes from inspiring leaders like Oprah Winfrey, Eleanor Roosevelt and Lady Gaga along with Lesley's own quotes. We all need a daily dose of motivation and inspiration and this book will give you 101 days of positivity to lift you up and help you have a positive attitude.

$24.95 Retail

Powerhouse Natasha Duswalt has put together these empowering and uplifting stories by women from all walks of life who have overcome challenges, solved problems and changed their lives for the better. This book will help you find your own inner strength, empowerment, and resilience. Real stories from real women like NY Times Best-Selling Author, Dr. Barbara De Angelis, the Queen of Sales Conversion, Lisa Sasevich, co-founder of Beyond Diet, Isabel De Los Rios, the owner of FrankieB. Jeans, Daniella Clarke & Award-Winning International Speaker, Lesley Nardini.

MOTIVATE AND INSPIRE OTHERS!
Share These Books

RETAIL $14.95

SPECIAL QUANTITY DISCOUNTS
On Any Combination of Book Titles

5-20 Books	10% Discount
21-99 Books	15% Discount
100-499 Books	20% Discount
500-599 Books	40% Discount
1,000+ Books	60% Discount

LESLEY NARDINI IS THE IDEAL PROFESSIONAL SPEAKER FOR YOUR NEXT EVENT!

Any organization that wants to develop their people to become EXTRAORDINARY and GET RESULTS needs to hire Lesley for a keynote speech and/or corporate training and coaching.

TO CONTACT AND BOOK LESELY TO SPEAK:
www.LesleyNardini.com
Email: Info@LesleyNardini.com
503-360-4604

DEDICATION

This is dedicated to all the amazing people who have inspired me, and continue to inspire me, to be a be a better person. I'm so grateful for fabulous friends and phenomenal family, especially my husband Carlo and my kids, Lorenzo and Cara. Your love and support are what keep me going and motivate me to be the best version of myself.

CONTENTS

ACKNOWLEDGMENTS

This book would not be complete without acknowledging the leaders and mentors who've inspired me and taught me the lessons that have helped me to have an incredible life. There are so many and these people are at the top of my list: Tony Robbins, Jack Canfield, Mark Victor Hansen, Les Brown, Brian Tracy, Mary Morrisey, Kevin Harrington, Maya Angelou, Craig Duswalt, Larry Broughton, Matt Brauning Zig Ziglar, Matt Brauning, Stephen Covey and Oprah Winfrey.

"Yesterday ended last night.
Today is a brand new day."
~Zig Ziglar

Chapter 1
Start Your Morning Strong

How you do anything is how you do life! How you start your morning has everything to do with how your day goes. One of the best ways to develop and maintain a positive attitude is by making sure to start your day off on the right foot. Develop a morning routine that empowers you and feeds your mind. The most successful people in the world are people who have a purposeful morning routine that puts them in control of their day.

I get asked all the time about how I'm able to maintain so much balance in my life. Here's how:
- On Sunday night I plan out my whole week starting with what's most important to me.
- I practice a powerful AM/PM routine.

Make it a habit to wake up just 15 minutes earlier in the morning so that you can do something that will get your mind in the right place. Journaling, yoga, power questions, meditation and/or prayer are all powerful habits that will change the course of your day which will change the course of your life. The things you do today will impact how your life will be 1 year from now. As you go through the chapters of this book, I'll share with you some of the tools and techniques I've learned and practiced over the years...the things that have helped me to be successful and have the life of my dreams.

"*The most pathetic person in the world is someone who has sight but no vision.*"
~Helen Keller

Chapter 2
Create a Vision Board

Having a vision board is a powerful, amazing tool that helps you have the life you want. Studies show that the pictures you see in your mind program your subconscious to attract more of that into your life. Your mind doesn't know the difference from something that's real or imagined. If you want to create something new in your life, it's critical that you are intentional about what you focus on. I have been creating vision boards on a regular basis for more than 20 years. At first, I was skeptical about whether or not it would work however, I've had so many of my visions come true that I'm convinced of the power of vision boards.

When you create your vision board, first write down your 3 main goals for the year ahead. Next get several magazines that appeal to you. I like to have magazines with the themes of Travel, Fitness, Lifestyle and Fashion. Next, you'll want to set a mood that's inspiring. Put on some great music, light some candles, pour a glass of champagne (or green tea) and start perusing the pages of the magazines. As you flip through the pages, cut out any pictures or words that appeal to you. It's ok, in fact it's great, to have way more pictures and words than you will need. Next step is to start arranging these on your board. It's more effective if you group pictures in themes like having all health/fitness pictures in a group but this is not mandatory.

I also find it really effective to attend a vision board party with a leader who knows how to help you get the most out of your vision board experience.

If you want to do yours on your own (I've done many on my own) I recommend searching for Jack Canfield's vision board video on YouTube. Give it a go and watch how your vision board changes your focus, helps you feel more positive and moves your life in a different direction.

"*Keep your heart clear and transparent, and you will never be bound. A single disturbed thought creates ten thousand distractions.*"

~*Ryokan*

Chapter 3
Meditation/Prayer

Meditation and prayer are powerful practices that bring calm, focus and peace of mind when practiced on a regular basis. Meditation and prayer help to focus your mind on the things that are most important in your life.

When you are in the habit of meditating and/or praying on a daily basis, you will notice a huge difference in how your days unfold. This practice helps you to set your intentions for the day and boosts your strength, courage and confidence to tackle whatever life hands you.

Often when I talk with people about meditation, they say that it's hard to find the time to fit this in to their lives. Remember that meditation and prayer can be effective with just 10 minutes a day. I love the quote that says, "When you are busy, meditate for ½ hour. If you're too busy for that, meditate for 1 hour." Meditation and prayer give you the mental space, focus and clarity you need to weed out the activities that are neither productive nor leading you to the life you want to have.

We now live in a world where we are constantly bombarded with all sorts of information (a majority of it being negative) from multiple sources and multiple electronic gadgets. This constant barrage of information can clutter your mind with nonsense and negativity that will impact your mood and your life. Because of this it's even more critical than ever to take the time to clear your mind so that you will be in control of your thoughts.

One of the easiest ways I know to make sure you can fit this habit into your life is to put a reminder on your bathroom mirror and/or night table. I also like to use the Headspace app. It's a free app that you can put on your phone and it gives you numerous options for daily meditation along with instructions on how to get the most out of it.

Meditation and prayer help you to clear the clutter in your brain and in your life so that you are free to create the life of your dreams.

"Yoga is not about tightening your ass. It's about getting your head out of it"
                    ~Eric Paskel

Chapter 4
Practice Yoga

There are a multitude of health benefits to practicing yoga. Movement of any kind does so much for your mood that it's imperative to find time and make time to move your body on a regular basis. When you exercise, your body releases endorphins in your system that elevate mood. I call them your body's own natural happy pill. Many people who experience mild depression have been able to overcome their depression by exercising regularly.

Yoga adds another element that helps you build strength both physically and mentally. Some people mistakenly think that Yoga is a spiritual practice and, while it can feel spiritual for some people, it's much more about mental focus. Yoga also helps you improve balance, core strength and muscle tone. I don't always take the time to put yoga into my routine but when I do it makes a huge difference in how I feel mentally and physically.

As I write this chapter, I'm currently going through a rough patch. My husband and I are relocating to a new state, which is both exciting and scary, and we recently lost one of our dogs when he was attacked by a neighbor dog. I'm feeling a huge amount of loss and grief at the moment and one of the things I have added back into my routine is daily yoga. I know it will make a huge difference in my mindset and my ability to cope with the big changes in my life.

Take this on for the next 30 days and notice what a difference it makes in your life. You can attend at a yoga studio and/or go online to get yoga sessions for free. And there are several different types of yoga available, from gentle stretching to power yoga to hot yoga. That hot yoga is incredible! Even 15 minutes a day will make a difference. I'd love to hear from you about how this makes a difference in your life.

"A good goal is like strenuous exercise—it makes you stretch."

~Mary Kay Ash

Chapter 5
Stretch Yourself

Years ago (in the 80s) I taught modeling school for Barbizon International. I loved every minute of it and met the most amazing people in the process. The students at the school were mostly teenage girls and occasionally we would have a male student or a grown-up woman. One such student was Isabelle who was in her 70s. I adored Isabelle and still remember her to this day. I was so impressed with how beautiful and vibrant she was as a mature woman. In my 20s, at the time, I had not met any women in their 70s who looked as beautiful and vibrant as Isabelle. One of the things she said to me that really stood out is the importance of developing and practicing healthy habits practiced on a daily basis. This sounds so simple, but it made a huge impression on me.

Among other things she said that every single morning, before getting out of bed, she always did stretching exercises. Later in life when I became a fitness instructor I learned about the health benefits of stretching. It improves circulation, oxygen flow, flexibility and muscle strength.

This chapter is about the importance of stretching yourself both physically and mentally. When you push yourself and stretch out of your comfort zone this is what helps you to stay healthy, vibrant and fully alive.

In the previous chapter I talked about the challenge of uprooting and moving to another state. One of the reasons my husband and I decided to make this move, besides a really nice job opportunity for him, is because we are committed to always stretching ourselves and living life to the fullest. It would have been so easy to stay safe and comfortable in the home we loved with our friends and family nearby but, we decided it would be better for us long term to get out of the comfort zone and stretch ourselves.

When you do this you might be surprised that your bold action will inspire someone else along the way. Not long after we decided to move some of our dearest friends decided to relocate to a new place after 25 years in the same house. My girlfriend told me that uprooting was far more difficult than she thought it would be but our example had inspired her and gave her the courage to make the move.

Always be committed to stretch yourself physically and mentally on a regular basis and you will be amazed at how this improves your attitude and your life.

"Thousands have lived without love, not one without water."
~W. H. Auden

Chapter 6
Drink More Water

Oh Mama! Who hasn't heard this one before? This is one of those pieces of advice that I hear over and over again and have taught this thousands of times myself and yet....I still find myself slacking off when it comes to drinking water. Like any habit, this is one that takes some effort to implement but the benefits are worth the effort. One thing that helps me drink more water is to put a cup on my night table to make it easy to drink first thing in the morning.

When you do this, you will be **amazed** at the impact it has on your physical and mental well-being. Your body is made up of about 70% water therefore when you are properly hydrated everything just works better. Think of it like making sure your car has the proper amount of oil to run efficiently.

Good hydration not only helps your organs work better, it also gives your brain mental clarity and helps you think more clearly. Drinking water keeps your skin glowing, helps you sleep better and, as a bonus, it helps to curb your appetite. How do you know you're getting enough? When your urine is almost clear, that's when you know. The health benefits of drinking 8-10 glasses of water each day are so tremendous that it's worth developing this habit.

"Always remember, your focus determines your reality."
~George Lucas

Chapter 7
Make a TaDa List

Make a WHAT list? Make a TaDa list! You know how when a magician does something magical there is always a "TaDa"! Making a TaDa list every day will magically make things appear in your life. My friend Larry Broughton taught me about the TaDa list. He said that when he was going through a rough patch in his life he decided to implement a few habits to help him change his focus and get his life on track. He said that the one habit that helped him the most was a TaDa list. At the end of every day he would write down 5 things that went well that day. Some days he would have to search for the smallest things to put on the list, but he would always come up with 5 things. So, I decided to implement this one habit with amazing results.

Last year my husband and I went through a rough patch in our relationship which happens in a lot of long-term relationships. We did several things to help us revive our marriage. One of the things we started doing is creating a TaDa list together in bed just before we go to sleep. It has been incredible how this one thing has helped us focus on all that is good in our relationship.

Making a TaDa List at the end of every day helps your mind focus on what's going well in your life. Several of my coaching clients have commented on how this one habit has helped them focus and feel more accomplished.

Whatever you focus on is what expands so when you focus on what's working well you will start to see more of that and, by default, you will create more of that. As a bonus, when you do this right before going to sleep, your subconscious will work on this while you're sleeping to magnify the success in your life.

Creating your TaDa list is a simple but powerful way to focus your thinking in a new way. Just do it!! You'll be amazed at the results.

"We cannot solve our problems with the same thinking we used when we created them."

~Albert Einstein

Chapter 8
Get Rid of ALL Your Problems

Would you like a simple tool to help you get rid of ALL your problems? You may be thinking this is impossible, but I assure you, when you go through this one simple exercise you will see that it's entirely possible to eliminate ALL of your problems. More importantly, you will have a powerful tool to help you effectively manage your problems and find solutions quickly.

I learned this technique many years ago when I was in direct sales for a cosmetics and image company. After using this tool numerous times in my own life I was blown away by the results I got. Because it's so amazing I decided to start adding this into my own seminars. The stories I've heard from people who have used this have been incredible. I've met people who've had huge breakthroughs and found solutions to problems that they had been dealing with for years. I've also met people who were able to find relief and new perspective on incredibly traumatic events in their lives. These experiences confirmed for me how very effective this can be when you use what I call "The List of 20". You will need a piece of paper and a pen to do this short but powerful exercise.

The step by step process starts here so go grab your pen and paper and get ready to get rid of all your problems.

Step 1: At the top left of your paper write the word "PROBLEM" with a line next to it, like this.

PROBLEM: _____

Step 2: Write down a problem you are currently facing. Pick the one that is weighing you down the most.

Step 3: Take your pen and scratch out the word "PROBLEM", then write the word "CHALLENGE". Just doing that will change the way you look at problems. The language and words you use have a huge impact on how you see the world. For most people the word "PROBLEM" conjures up heavy thoughts of burdens that can weigh you down and make you feel stuck. Train yourself to refocus and learn to look at problems as "CHALLENGES". That word is far more empowering and will put you in a resourceful state of mind that will help you more easily find solutions.

Step 4: Make a list of 20 things about this challenge that are "good". When I say "good", what I mean are 20 good things that can come out of this. For example, in one of my seminars there was a woman whose "challenge" was that her brother had been murdered just 10 months earlier. At first, she did not like the suggestion that there was anything "good" about this. However, as she shifted her focus and did the exercise what she found was there were many good things that could come from this tragic situation. For instance, it was a chance for her to strengthen her relationship with God and she knew that because she had gone through this situation, she would be able to help others who were facing the same challenge. She came to me in tears and said for the first time in 10 months she could breathe more easily. I encourage you to do this exercise and be sure to fill out all 20 spots. It's a very powerful exercise that will help you manage your ~~problems~~ *challenges* more effectively.

I would love to hear from you about how this exercise has helped you. Please email me at info@lesleynardini.com to share your success!

"Filling your mind with negativity will never give you a great life."

~Lesley Nardini

Chapter 9
Turn Off the News

For the next 30 days, I challenge you to go on a complete **News Fast**. Eliminate any and ALL news from your view for just 30 days. This is more challenging that it sounds because we now live in a day and age when we have 24-hour access to the news from multiple sources that are hard to turn off and tune out.

Whenever I teach this in my seminars inevitably someone will say, "But how will I know what's going on in the world?" I assure you that even when you're on a "News Fast" you will still hear about the important things. The news will get to you one way or another but, what I've found is, when I'm on a "News Fast" I hear about important things in a less sensational and frightening way. If I want to or need to know more I will then go and **read** about it (don't watch it, just read) from a news source that I know is reputable and balanced.

To do this effectively you will have to turn off news notifications on all your electronic devices, so the news isn't popping up in your face all the time. I had to ask someone to help me figure this out but it's not hard. You will have to be disciplined about how you use social media platforms. This is also much harder than it seems. Social media are designed to "hook" us in to look at them regularly.

There is an addictive quality to social media and phone apps. You must approach this the same way you would approach a detox of your body. You are detoxing your mind.

One of my coaching clients was complaining to me about how much the news was getting to her, especially politics. I encouraged her to go on a news fast for 30 days. At first, she didn't think she could give up her addiction so she started by recording the news so that she could watch it and fast forward through the parts that were upsetting. That helped enough that she decided not to watch at all. She was excited to report back to me that she felt calmer, her blood pressure went down and she was nicer to her husband. Now THAT is taking control of your life instead of letting the news control you.

It's challenging but the pay offs are incredible. You will be happier, calmer, able to think more clearly and have way more control of your life.

"Self-care is giving the world the best of you, instead of what's left of you."
~Katie Reed

Chapter 10
Get a Massage

For the past few years I've been getting massages about once a month and I can't tell you how much my life has improved by doing this one simple thing. Getting a full body massage has so many health benefits that it's worth the investment of time and money to add this to your self-care routine.

Numerous studies and health experts agree that massage can have a huge impact on your health and wellbeing. The following list shows a few of the things that massage can help improve:

- Anxiety and Depression
- Diabetes
- Chronic Pain
- Back Pain
- Arthritis Pain
- Better Posture
- Headache Relief
- Fibromyalgia Pain
- Lowers Blood Pressure
- Improved Blood Circulation
- Improved Flexibility
- Enhances Athletic Performance
- Helps You Sleep Better
- Treat Sports Injuries

If you're on a budget here are a few ideas to help fit this into your life financially:

1. Many health insurance plans now cover part or all of massage therapy as preventive care. On my plan I pay just $25 per session.
2. Some massage therapists offer discounts when purchasing multiple massages at once.
3. Search for a massage therapist who is willing to trade services with you.
4. Massage training facilities often offer discounts so that therapists-in-training can get practice hours.

With so many health benefits why would you not add this into your self-care routine? Remember that when you take good care of yourself, you're more productive, more energetic and you will live a longer happier life. It's hard to give anything to others when your tank is on empty so be sure you're doing something like massage to fill your tank so you will have more to give to those around you.

"There are shortcuts to happiness and dancing is one of them."

~Vicki Baum

Chapter 11
Dance Like Nobody's Watching

Have you wondered why the TV shows "Dancing With the Stars" and "So You Think You Can Dance" have become so popular? Dancing is a joyful celebration of life that lifts your mood, even when you're just watching on television. When you take it to the next level and participate, it positively lights up your world. Dancing improves your life in 3 primary ways – physical health, social interaction and mental acuity.

A 2014 article published by Berkley Wellness, at Berkley University, supports the health benefits of dance. It sites a review done in the European Journal of Physical Rehab Medicine saying that dancing can even help people with Parkinson's disease. The physical benefits are improved balance, range of motion and muscle strength. Some of the emotional benefits of dancing include improved mood and self-confidence. Anytime you do any kind of physical exercise your body releases endorphins which always boosts your mood. Dance has also been shown to reduce anxiety and depression while boosting body image and coping skills. In addition, it helps sharpen your mind. When you're learning new dance steps and you combine that with music your mental acuity improves.

For many people who love to dance, the social interaction is what they love the most. It's a positive, healthy activity to do with your significant other. If you're single, it's a great way to meet other people. I often hear single people complaining that they don't know how to meet other single people, other than online dating sites. I always recommend joining a club, organization and/or classes with activities you love to do. This is the perfect way to meet people with shared interests and usually, people who are active & social, tend to be healthier all around. I know this is a generalization, but seriously, the odds go up when you're meeting people while doing fun, healthy activities.

Some people shy away from dancing due to a bad experience in junior high or simply out of embarrassment for not being coordinated. My philosophy is to be bold, courageous and willing to try something new. Whenever you take something new, that pushes you out of your comfort zone you always grow more courageous. Whether you choose salsa, tango, waltzing, square dancing or line dancing, have fun with it and watch how your mood and your life improve.

"The quality of your life comes down to the quality of the questions you ask yourself on a daily basis."

~Tony Robbins

Chapter 12
Power Questions

I learned this lesson from Tony Robbins several years ago and it remains one of the most powerful techniques I've learned to dramatically change my life. When I was in my early 20s, I was struggling with everything in my life. My dad had passed away suddenly which absolutely devastated me and compounded some of the other issues in my life. The unbelievable pain and my inability to deal with my grief enhanced all my other insecurities. I was a mess and my life was a mess in every possible way. After a great deal of pain and struggle and making some very bad decisions, I decided I wanted to turn my life around. While sitting up late one night I came across an informercial touting a personal development program by Tony Robbins called *30 Days to Personal Power*. I took a chance and invested in the program. I learned so many amazing tools that helped me to turn my life around. The power questions especially helped me to define and focus on the things that were most important to me. And they will do the same for you.

This super simple tool will take you just 2-3 minutes to complete. It works best to do it first thing in the morning. All you need are 3 index cards or even a plain piece of paper will work. On each card write down 3 questions to ask yourself right after you wake up. The questions should be focused on 3 areas of your life that you want to improve. So, what is it for you? Is it your health? Your finances? Your career? What about family and relationships? What's the area of your life that gives you the most anxiety in your life? This is where to look because, most likely, your anxiety stems from the fact that this is an important part of your life that's not working well. If you didn't care about it, you wouldn't have anxiety.

Next, identify 3 main areas that you would like to improve in your life then form the questions to ask yourself to help you change the way you think about this topic. Here are examples. When I was struggling in my early 20s the 3 things that created the most stress were my financial situation, my marriage and my weight. I had a lot of fear and anxiety around these 3 topics, so I came up with 3 questions to help me focus my attention on solutions.

1. What is one thing I can do today to improve my marriage and family?
2. What is one thing I can do today to improve my financial situation?
3. What is one thing I can do today to improve my health and fitness?

After formulating your questions then each morning you write down your answers to the questions. You must come up with answers, just one action step you can take to make an improvement TODAY on this area of your life.

When you take small steps every single day it adds up to a changed life over time. Doing this also helps you retrain your mind to focus on solutions. It's magical how powerful this one simple tool will be in changing your life.

What are your 3 questions???

1. _____

2. _____

3. _____

"*Let us forgive each other. Only then will we live in peace.*"
~Leo Tolstoy

Chapter 13
The Power of Forgiveness

Of all the things I've learned that have helped me to heal and become a better person, forgiveness is the most powerful lesson of all. The primary benefit in forgiving someone who has wronged you is that it frees you up to move on with your life in a powerful way. When you hold on to the anger and resentment that comes from being hurt by a friend or loved one, that anger and resentment becomes a ball and chain that will weigh you down and get in the way of living a happy fulfilled life.

I once heard someone say that staying angry at someone who's hurt you is like drinking poison and hoping it will kill the other person. Staying angry at someone, while sometimes justified, will only poison you if you hang on to it for a long time.

Years back I read the book *A Return to Love* by Marianne Williamson. I recently picked up the revised edition to remind me of the powerful lessons I learned the first time I read it. This book had a profound effect on me, giving me insights that changed my perspective on the power of love. In the book she shares a phrase that I've since used to free me up from a great deal of hurt. To do this for yourself, first think of a person who has done something to cause you hurt, pain and/or anger.

Then insert that person's name into the blank space in this phrase:

"I love you _____, I forgive you and release you to the Holy Spirit."

I have modified this when I have felt hurt by people who are close to me, like my husband or a close family member:

"I love you _____, I forgive you and release my feelings to the Holy Spirit."

Say this over and over again until you feel the release of and hurt and anger you have from a past situation. This does not have to be done in person. You can even do this with people who have passed away. Remember that forgiveness is meant to set *you* free from past hurts so that you can move on and live your life to the fullest. I believe that the act of sending love and forgiveness to someone who has hurt you goes a long way to healing not just yourself, but also the world around you.

"Take care of your body. It's the only place you have to live."
~Jim Rohn

Chapter 14
Exercise

The benefits of regular physical exercise can not be stated enough! We've all heard it our whole lives and it's true. If you are not already doing some form of physical exercise on a regular basis, do whatever you have to do to add this in to your life. If you already have this habit, congratulations!! You are doing one of the most powerful things you can possibly do to help you have a winning attitude.

Here are benefits of physical exercise:
1. It activates and releases endorphins into your system which elevates your mood. I call this your body's natural happy pills.
2. Sweating during exercise helps to detox your body.
3. Cardio exercise burns calories.
4. Resistance or weight training helps build muscle which has all sorts of benefits.
    a. Did you know that building muscles increases your metabolism and fat-burning even more than cardio?
    b. Also, weight training improves bone density so that, as you age, your bones will be stronger and less brittle.
    c. Weight training is what gives your body definition, strength and balance.
    d. It also helps you have fewer back and neck issues. When your muscles are

strong, they support the rest of your body to function well.

Cardio and strength training are equally important. Think of it like using 2 oars when rowing a boat. Using both oars will help you get to your destination more quickly.

If you're not already in the habit, start by adding in just 10-15 minutes of some movement in the morning. Doing this at the start of your day gets your blood flowing and oxygenates your brain which helps you think more clearly throughout the day.

If you're still resistant to this, or feel like you just don't have the time, you will be more motivated if you can connect the benefits of exercise to the things that are most important in your life. For many people, family is what matters most. For me, getting strong and healthy means that I will live longer and be more energetic to support my family and enjoy a great life with them. *What is your primary motivation for exercising?*

"I can shake off everything as I write; my sorrows disappear, my courage is reborn."
        ~Anne Frank

Chapter 15
Journaling

Several years ago, I read an amazing book called *The Artist's Way* by Julia Cameron. ***Side note:*** when I decided to read this book, it was after I had heard about it from 3 different people in 3 very different situations in a short period of time. I believe that when you come across something 3 times it's a sign. Pay attention!! The universe is trying to tell you something.

In the book *The Artist's Way*, one of the main components is the importance and value of journaling every morning. By journaling and putting all your thoughts on paper, you are clearing the clutter from your mind so that you can start your day with a clean slate and a clear head. With a fresh perspective on your day you will be far more productive and it will be much easier to find solutions to whatever challenges come your way. I've found that it's much easier to feel strong and courageous when I'm journaling on a regular basis.

Journaling also gives you a tool to work through any issues that may be weighing on you. Something magical happens when you transfer your thoughts on to paper so that you can see them from a different perspective. In *The Artist's Way*, Julia recommends that you don't read or even keep your journal pages. It's meant to dump your thoughts out of your head so that you can clear the clutter and take on your day with a clear mind. Most of the stuff that runs around in our brains is not necessary to functioning well anyway. In fact, most of our thoughts are negative and will get in the way of you having your best life.

Just the other day, one of my dear friends told me she has been journaling consistently, every single day, for the past 6 months. She said this one simple practice has helped her to stay focused in a positive direction during a very challenging time in her life. I myself have experienced a great deal of transition and upheaval over the past year and my journaling practice is one of the main things that has helped me handle this transition with ease.

Adopt this one simple practice for the next 30 days and see the difference it will make in your life.

"Let food be thy medicine and medicine be thy food."
~Hippocrates

Chapter 16
More Fruits and Veggies

I'll be honest with you…of all the advice I have for you in this book, this is my least favorite and I resist this the most. I would much rather get my fruit from a nice glass of red wine than eating a bunch of grapes. However, I do know and appreciate how beneficial it is to eat fruits and vegetables on a daily basis. Fruits and vegetables have the highest concentration of vitamins, nutrients and antioxidants to feed your body than anything else you can put in your mouth. I've been reading a lot lately about how antioxidants can reverse damage done to your body, including sun damage to your skin.

I'll keep this chapter short and sweet because I'm pretty sure you've heard a million times how important this is to your health and well-being. Lately, I've been finding ways to make it as easy as possible to get more fruits and vegetables into my diet. Having your favorite fruits and veggies on hand that are easy to grab and go will make a difference. I've also recently discovered that there are many options in the frozen section to always have something on hand that's easy to whip up. I love the packages of "riced" cauliflower, broccoli and sweet potatoes and I love to add blueberries to my oatmeal. So yummy! *What can you do to bring more fruits & veggies into your diet?*

"Thoughts become things. If you see it in your mind, you will hold it in your hand."
~Bob Proctor

Chapter 17
Visualization & Affirmations

One of my favorite books is *Dare to Win* by Mark Victor Hansen. I read this book in preparation for the Mrs. Oregon International pageant in 1997. Up until that point I had tried and tried to win numerous pageants in the past. In every competition I had done previously, I had never even come close. I was never a runner up or a finalist and each time I "lost" I felt more and more like a failure. Despite all of the loss and failure, I persisted, and each time learned something about myself that I could apply to my life. Each time I worked to become a stronger, more polished version of myself. In 1997, I decided to try again, 20 years after my first pageant. This time around I came across the book *Dare to Win*. The title alone felt intriguing and a little scary to me. It made me realize that sometimes the thought of winning takes courage. It's a daring thing to want to win because, when you do accomplish your goal it puts you out in front, in a position where you are more visible. That can be scary.

Based on the things I learned from this book I knew that visualizing myself as the winner was a key factor to my success. I had to see myself already in that position. I had to believe with all my heart and soul that I could achieve that goal. I took on the challenge and for 6 months leading up to the pageant I visualized myself winning and created affirmations to support this goal. I heard my name being called and saw the crown being placed on my head. At first it felt weird but eventually it became comfortable. In fact, after a while, it became natural and normal. I saw this picture so much and said the words to myself so often that this image became ingrained in me. I *knew* I had what it takes to win. I believed it so strongly that, at a certain point, it didn't even matter if the judges agreed with me. In the end, they did, and I was crowned Mrs. Oregon International. For me, it was an amazing accomplishment that helped me grow to new levels of success in my life.

I'm 100% certain that affirming and visualizing myself winning was a key component to my success. I have applied these same concepts to achieve all sorts of amazing things that I never thought were possible.

What is one big goal you want to accomplish? Start now to visualize yourself already having achieved that goal. Write that down in the affirmative and recite your affirmation. Doing this at night before you fall asleep will lock the image into your subconscious mind. You will be amazed at what happens in your life.

"Stand guard at the door of your mind."

~Tony Robbins

Chapter 18
What Are You Feeding Your Mind?

One of the most important aspects to having a winning attitude is to be conscientious about what you feed your mind.

Think of your attitude and mindset like a garden. If you want to have a beautiful, thriving garden you have to put in the effort. A wonderful garden does not happen all by itself and neither does a winning attitude. Also, to keep your garden healthy and thriving you must maintain it on a regular basis. If you neglect your garden the weeds will come right back in and take over. Similarly, if you don't put in the time and effort to have a strong healthy mindset, negativity, pessimism and cynicism (the weeds) will come right in and take over your life.

If you knew that someone was adding a drop of poison to your food every day, would you stand by and take it? Of course not! And yet, so many people allow negative information to poison their mind on a daily basis. When you listen to the news and/or hang around with complainers you are allowing poison to drip into your mind. Make a vow right now to "tend your garden" and start taking care of the information you feed your mind. If you will follow these simple steps for the next 30 days, you will be amazed at the difference in how you feel. Strengthening your mind and your attitude will increase happiness, decrease anxiety, help you to be more productive and have better relationships. You will feel less irritated by other people and you won't get upset in traffic. Do these next steps for 30 days and watch how your life transforms:

1. ***Turn off the news.*** Don't watch or listen to the news for 30 days. The news is designed to capture your attention by focusing on the worst things that are happening in the world. It gives you a distorted and scary view of what's really happening. I promise that even when you ignore the news you will still hear about the important stories.

2. ***Read/listen to motivational, inspirational books*** in the morning and at night just before you go to bed. When you do this on your commute you strengthen your mind which helps you be more productive at work. When you put positive information in your mind just before bed you will sleep more peacefully.

3. ***Find 5 things you're grateful for.*** Just before going to sleep write down 5 things you're grateful for in your life. Whatever you think about before you go to sleep gets locked into your subconscious mind which helps you bring more of that into your life.

4. ***Don't complain!*** If you're in the habit of complaining a lot, it will take some effort to undo this habit. Catch yourself when you find yourself complaining and force yourself to find a solution. As you change this habit you will feel less like a victim and more in control of your life.

5. ***Stand Guard at the Door of Your Mind!*** I love this phrase that I learned from Tony Robbins. He is masterful at teaching how to take control of your thoughts and develop a healthy mindset. I highly recommend any of his material to further your personal growth.

"When you have goals, you are creating your life instead of reacting to it."

~Lesley Nardini

Chapter 19
Set 101 Goals

I started my journey of personal development in my early 20s. During that time my life was a mess. I struggled tremendously after my dad's sudden death and I lacked a sense of purpose or direction. One of the things that helped give me direction was becoming a member of Toastmasters, an organization that helps people develop communication and leadership skills. The meetings are structured, and I learned the value of having clear goals to reach milestones in the organization. The growth I experienced sparked an interest in personal development that inspired me to study great speakers like Tony Robbins, Brian Tracy, Zig Ziglar, Napoleon Hill and Jack Canfield.

After consuming info from numerous books, audio programs and seminars I started to see a pattern to the "formula for success". I knew that if I would just follow a few simple rules and develop certain habits I could have a successful, happy life. One of the rules that is taught in every single program on success is the importance of goal setting. If there is only one nugget of information I can give you in this book, goal-setting is that one principle I hope you take away. I can't state strongly enough how important this is to your success in every aspect of life.

One of the best books I've read on this subject is *The Aladdin Factor* by Jack Canfield and Mark Victor Hansen. The book lays out a simple process to follow that will help you get clear about your goals and vision. It teaches the importance of creating a list of 101 goals. When you have a lot of goals you have something that's always pulling you forward.

After reading this book for the first time in 1996 there was a story of a couple that wrote out a detailed goal and vision of their dream home and how everything that had written down, including price and closing date, had come true for them when they got their dream home. This was so inspiring that my husband and I decided to do this process. In 1996 we created and wrote down our dream home goals, including pictures on a vision board, and a closing date of June 2000. On April 1, 2000 we moved into our dream home on the street that we wanted to live on, a vision that had been created 4 years earlier. I have so many other stories of all the amazing things that have happened in our life as a result of goal setting. It absolutely works.

When I first read about having a list of 101 goals it felt daunting and impossible to create such a big list. But once you get going your mind opens to all the possibilities. Set aside an hour, light a candle, put on some uplifting music and start writing. Your list will include everything you want to accomplish from small mundane easy tasks (clean out that junk drawer!) all the way up to your dream car, dream house and dream vacation. Think about ways that you want to contribute to organizations that are important to you. What are your financial goals, health & fitness goals, relationship goals, career goals, activities, hobbies and fun goals? There are so many possibilities. Just open your mind and think out of the box when creating your list. There is no wrong way to do this. You will be amazed at the magical power of writing down your goals!!

"Each of us needs to withdraw from the cares which will not withdraw from us."
~Maya Angelou

Chapter 20
Take More Vacations

Life is meant to be lived! Somewhere in my early years I made the decision to live life to the fullest. I'm not quite sure what sparked this decision, but I do remember thinking to myself as a teenager, "Life is short and since we're here anyway, we might as well make the most of it." After my dad passed away at the young age of 52 this philosophy became even more relevant for me. Taking vacations is an important part of a life well lived. Almost everyone I talk to agrees that taking time off to enjoy beautiful scenery, nature and/or adventure is essential to having a positive outlook on life.

Vacationing renews your soul and relaxes your mind so that you can come back to work with a new perspective. Essentially it fills your tank so that you have more to give to others. If you're always running on empty, not only will you get burned out, you will also have a harder time being fully present for your work and life commitments.

Taking vacations does not have to be expensive or lengthy. A weekend camping trip can refresh your soul and it's something you can do more regularly. If you dream of taking 2 weeks in Europe or Hawaii start by writing down that goal. Create a vision board with your dream destination and put it in a place where you will see it every day. It's amazing how this works to pull you towards your dream and find the time and resources to make it happen.

One time in a seminar I was conducting I had everyone in the room write down a few goals, including a dream vacation spot. After discussing the power of written goals, one person in the room said she had done this 5 years before, dreaming about a trip to Ireland. She said when she first wrote this goal it was so outrageous to her, she did not see how it would ever happen. It was a dream that was so meaningful to her that she stayed with it. Three years after setting the goal and vision, she inherited some money that allowed her to take her dream trip with her family. If she had not created the goal, she may have ended up blowing her inheritance on something less meaningful to her. Having the vision made it crystal clear to her exactly what she would do with the inheritance. Taking her vacation was something that renewed her soul and created incredible memories that would stay with her for life.

Take more vacations!

"When we clear the physical clutter from our lives, we literally make way for inspiration to enter."

~Julia Cameron

Chapter 21
Clear the Clutter

There are two very important reasons to work on clearing the clutter in your life:
1. Habits
2. Clarity

Several years ago, I was sitting in a Jim Rohn seminar when he said, "If you can put your clothes away at night, you can become a millionaire." This statement caught my attention for 2 reasons. First of all, I really liked the idea of becoming a millionaire (or at least being financially secure) and secondly, at the time I was not putting my clothes away at night. I thought to myself, "Is it really that easy?" He went on the explain what he really meant, that becoming a millionaire is a matter of developing certain habits. It's that simple! Therefore, if you can develop the habit of putting your clothes away at night, you can develop the habits that will make you financially secure, or a millionaire if you want.

That simple concept excited me and that very night, when I went home, I started the habit of putting away my clothes every single night. I did it long enough that it became a habit that I have to this day. I got excited! I then started working on other habits that eventually developed into practicing the habits that would lead to financial security and now, millionaire status.

There's another phrase I've heard many times, "A cluttered desk equals a cluttered mind." This quote is attributed to former Texas Attorney General McCraw. To be fair, Albert Einstein said, "If a cluttered desk is a sign of a cluttered mind then what does an empty desk indicate?" I've also found an article stating that a messy desk is a sign of genius. Looking at both sides of this argument, combined with my personal experience, I believe that positive habits and clean spaces lead to more clarity and productivity than having a messy environment.

I happen to love the study stating that a messy desk is a sign of genius because I am, by nature, not a super organized person. I honestly believe that some of us have that in our nature and some of us have to work hard to have an organized, clutter-free environment. I have worked hard to develop the habits that create a clutter-free desk, closet, kitchen and home. My life definitely works better when my surroundings are free of clutter.

In my seminars I encourage people to start by clearing out just one "junk drawer". Another place to de-clutter is your closet. Take just 10 minutes to get rid of 10 things in your closet that you haven't worn in the past year. I've also read about the importance of keeping your purse organized and free of clutter. The philosophy is that this is part of honoring and respecting your finances. I'm so committed to having financial peace of mind that I decided to heed this advice and make sure my purse is always neat and clean.

You will be absolutely amazed at how developing these simple habits will clear your mind and make room in your life for the abundance you deserve.

"A good coach can change a game; a great coach can change a life."

~John Wooden

Chapter 22
Hire a Good Coach

Michael Jordan is considered to be one of the very best basketball players to have ever played the game. He mastered his craft and had world class knowledge about the game of basketball. He credits his coaches for helping him get to that level of expertise. Here's what's even more interesting about his achievements. Even after he reached the pinnacle of success, he continued to have coaches that helped him stay sharp and fine tune his skills. He understood what all successful people know. In order to reach high levels of success you **must** have help to get there. In order to be above average and achieve anything of significance, you must have someone who will coach you and push you to excel.

For the past 25 years I have had some form of coaching to help me excel in various parts of my life. One of the best examples of this is during the times when I have trained to get in shape for my pageant competitions. As a 20-year fitness instructor I have accumulated a great deal of knowledge about what it takes to get, and stay, in physical shape. I know exactly what to do to get in shape, but I've noticed that just having the knowledge doesn't get me in shape. I still have to put in the time, effort and sweat to build muscle and burn calories. I've also noticed that sometimes I'm really bored with doing the same routine and I frequently don't want to put in the time. Even though I know what to do I will hire a trainer to help me reach my goals. A coach offers you a different perspective and, if the coach is good, they will push you much harder than you will push yourself. They will motivate you when you feel discouraged and want to quit.

If you truly want to achieve anything great in life—great relationships, career success, financial security, fulfill a lifelong dream, peak fitness and vitality—it's essential to hire a coach. Besides the motivation and push a coach provides, when you pay you pay attention. There's an added measure of motivation when you have invested money to help you achieve success.

There are examples of people who have achieved great things with out a coach however, these examples are rare. If you're not to the point where you can afford a coach yet, you can get virtual coaching through audio programs that are affordable and sometimes free. Whichever way you decide to do it, make sure to get a coach to help you have the life of your dreams.

"Surround yourself with only people who are going to lift you higher."

~Oprah Winfrey

Chapter 23
Join a Mastermind Group

In the last chapter I talked about the importance of having a good coach. When you join a mastermind group, in addition to coaching, you will accelerate your success and achievement of your goals. Besides having numerous coaches, both virtually and live, I've also been involved with numerous mastermind groups over the past 20 years.

These are the benefits you will experience when you join a mastermind group.
1. Accountability
2. Motivation
3. Fresh perspective
4. New ideas
5. The power of group dynamics

Let's take a look at each of these.

Accountability: When you have big scary goals that push you out of your comfort zone, it's so easy to give up on your goals and dreams at the first sign of difficulty. I promise you, when you have a big scary goal, you will face difficulty and obstacles on the way to getting there. When you are part of a mastermind group, you are surrounded by supportive people who will lift you up and encourage you to stick with your dreams. I've also noticed that when I tell other people about my goals, I'm much more likely to stick with them. That's what accountability will do for you. That's what a mastermind will do for you.

Motivation: The root word of motivation is motive. When you're motivated you are connected to the **why** behind your goals which helps you stay on track when you get discouraged. When you join a mastermind group and share your goals with other successful people, they will remind you why you decided to pursue your goals in the first place. Another benefit is that other people can see your blind spots more easily than you can see them yourself. This is the essence of motivation and we need others to help us stay on track.

Fresh Perspective: I can't tell you the number of times I've gotten "stuck" and discouraged when pursuing my goals. When you do big things without the help of others, it's easy to stagnate and give up. A mastermind group will help you see things from a new perspective that will push you to the next level of success.

New ideas: We often fail to see the genius in our own ideas. A mastermind group will help you to see, hear and feel when you have a great idea that resonates with people as well as giving you fresh ideas on how you can reach your goals.

The Power of Group Dynamics: The first time I joined a mastermind I was a little skeptical about whether it was worth it. I soon realized how powerful it is to be around a group of likeminded, successful people. The energy that is created when a group of people is thinking in a similar way is magical. One of my first mentors, Mark Victor Hansen, would hold up his index fingers to show that when 2 people come together the power increases to 11, instead of 2. Over and over again this has been proven to be true for me.

Check it out for yourself and remember, when you join a mastermind, it's important to go in with a mindset of giving and participating to the fullest. You get what you give in a mastermind.

"*It's what you learn after you know it all that counts.*"
~*John Wooden*

Chapter 24
Go to School in Your Car

In my profession as a speaker and seminar leader I constantly remind my audience members about the importance of continuous learning. The people who resist this message the most are the ones who struggle the most. The two biggest **excuses** I hear from people are they don't have the time and/or money to read or listen to educational, motivational, inspirational information. Notice I said that these are excuses, not valid reasons. Anyone can make the time to learn, grow and become better. In addition, there are now many very affordable, and in some cases free, options to get your hands on educational material that will help you grow and improve.

One of the easiest ways to find time is to have audio programs that you listen to while in your car. If you are spending even 15 minutes on your commute to work, that's 30 minutes per day which adds up to roughly 10 hours a month of time you can spend improving yourself. You can turn your car into your university and learn a whole new subject, skill or way of thinking. By choosing to listen to motivational, educational, inspirational information instead of the news, talk radio or music you are choosing how to program your thinking. By using your drive time wisely, you are taking control of your life and creating your life instead having someone else dictate how or what to think.

Successful people are not lucky. They do things differently than the average person. That's how you become above average, when you're willing to put in the extra effort and use your time wisely to help improve your life and the life of those around you. Take control of your life by using your drive time as an opportunity to make your life better.

"*Your level of success is in direct proportion to your willingness to get uncomfortable.*"

~*Lesley Nardini*

Chapter 25
Get Out of Your Comfort Zone

When I get on stage and speak to an audience, one of my goals is to make people uncomfortable. Now you might be asking yourself, "Why would she want to make people uncomfortable?" My primary goals are to educate and motivate people when I'm speaking and I also strive to bring just a little discomfort by challenging people to do something that's a little outside of the box. The reason I do this is because I know that discomfort is where the growth happens. The only way you grow and become stronger is when you do something that takes you out of your comfort zone, creating discomfort which helps you go to new levels of success.

For example, when I'm giving a seminar on leadership, I take people through an exercise where they practice how to give negative feedback to employees but do it in a positive way. Most people who are in leadership positions get zero to little training on how to give feedback in a way that people will listen, grow and take action to improve. The exercise I take people through often creates a lot of discomfort, mainly because it's not something they have ever done. People love the exercise and I remind them that when they go back to work and use the technique for the first time, they will most likely feel uncomfortable. I let them know to expect it and to stay with it until this new technique becomes comfortable.

The average person will walk away at the first sign of discomfort because it can be embarrassing or scary or frustrating or all of the above. Don't be average! When you recognize your discomfort and realize that it's what helps you to grow, you'll start to welcome it and stick with it until you have a new skill and a new way of being.

What's something you can do to face your fear, get uncomfortable and push through it to come out stronger on the other side? When you do this, you will be amazed at how courageous and confident you will feel.

"*Having a healthy, winning attitude takes effort, just as it takes effort to have a healthy body.*"

~Lesley Nardini

Chapter 26
Become a Junkie!

I was in my mid-twenties when I first started to study personal development programs. At that time my life was a huge mess. My husband and I got married very young and a few months after, my dad passed away suddenly of a heart attack. This was devastating to our whole family and I did not handle his death well. It put a huge strain on my marriage which was already fragile due to our inexperience and difficulty with good communication. We nearly got divorced a couple of times but somehow had the determination to work through our challenges.

I knew that I wanted to learn how to be a successful person in all aspects of my life including marriage, friendships, money, health, career, etc.... I also knew I could not accomplish this on my own. I wanted to do better but I just did not know how so I started the journey. As I mentioned earlier, the first program I invested in was Tony Robbin's *30 Days to Personal Power*. It was incredibly effective and helped me so much to make better decisions in my life. It helped me see the difficulties I faced in a different way which gave me freedom and options. What I also found is that the information would help me for awhile but then, as time went by, I would find myself reverting to some of my old habits. When that happened, I would go back to seminars, books and audio programs that would motivate me to keep improving and it always made a difference in how I felt.

When I would share my excitement with people around me, I sometimes was ridiculed for being a "motivation junkie". I would hear, "Why do you need that stuff? It's ridiculous." That was difficult to hear and sometimes made me want to quit, but I persisted. I knew that I wanted something more and I was determined to create my life on my own terms.

My "addiction" to personal development is absolutely 100% the reason for my success in life. It's what keeps me on track and focused when life gets hard. It's what helps me to stay positive in a negative world and to see the beauty in people when it's sometimes hard to see that. Being a "motivational junkie" is the best kind of addiction to have. The time is now to get on board and take control of your life!

ABOUT THE AUTHOR

Award-Winning international speaker and author, Lesley Nardini brings a unique blend of motivation, inspiration and success skills to your organization. She is America's leading expert on delivering exceptional customer service and is an authority on communication and influence.

Lesley's career has spanned 30+ years working with the public, primarily in the hospitality, fitness and banking industries, winning numerous awards for exceptional customer service.

Lesley majored in business and communications in college and has extensive ongoing training in professional speaking and communication skills. She has completed Anthony Robbins Mastery University as well as the Landmark Education Leadership Series. She is certified as a Jack Canfield Trainer and is also a certified NLP coach.

Lesley has given more than 1,000 speeches in front of more than 25,000 people and gotten rave reviews about her ability to engage audiences, create excitement and impart information that makes a difference. She has spoken all over the United States and in several countries as a keynote speaker and seminar leader for Fortune 500 companies.

A list of the companies she has spoken to include:

FAA	US Department of Transportation
Delta Airlines	Burpee Seeds
Oracle	The City of Los Angeles
Siemens	Northwestern Mutual
Johns Hopkins University	Shell Oil
Indiana Wesleyan University	US Department of Energy
US Army	Navajo Nation

Lesley began her speaking career as an image consultant and now helps people improve their total image from the inside out with her signature program called "Lead With Style: Package Yourself for Success". She knows that everything about you communicates a message and having a winning attitude is critical to projecting confidence and creating all the success and happiness you deserve in your life.

For more information and to book Lesley visit: https://LesleyNardini.com